I0669566

MY PERSONAL PASSWORD & INTERNET ADDRESSES BOOK

PASSWORD NOTEBOOK

ACTIVINOTES

Activinotes

DAILY JOURNALS, PLANNERS, NOTEBOOKS AND OTHER BLANK BOOKS

Website:_____
Username:_____
Password:_____
Hint:_____
Notes:

_____
_____
_____

Website:_____
Username:_____
Password:_____
Hint:_____
Notes:

_____
_____
_____

Website:_____
Username:_____
Password:_____
Hint:_____
Notes:

_____
_____
_____

Website:_____
Username:_____
Password:_____
Hint:_____
Notes:

_____
_____
_____

Website:_____
Username:_____
Password:_____
Hint:_____
Notes:

_____
_____

Website:_____
Username:_____
Password:_____
Hint:_____
Notes:

_____
_____
_____

Website:_____
Username:_____
Password:_____
Hint:_____
Notes:

_____
_____
_____

Website:_____
Username:_____
Password:_____
Hint:_____
Notes:

_____
_____
_____

Website:_____
Username:_____
Password:_____
Hint:_____
Notes:

_____
_____
_____

Website:_____
Username:_____
Password:_____
Hint:_____
Notes:

_____
_____

Website:_____
Username:_____
Password:_____
Hint:_____
Notes:
_____
_____
_____

Website:_____
Username:_____
Password:_____
Hint:_____
Notes:
_____
_____
_____

Website:_____
Username:_____
Password:_____
Hint:_____
Notes:
_____
_____
_____

Website:_____
Username:_____
Password:_____
Hint:_____
Notes:
_____
_____
_____

Website:_____
Username:_____
Password:_____
Hint:_____
Notes:
_____
_____
_____

Website:_____
Username:_____
Password:_____
Hint:_____
Notes:
_____
_____
_____

Website:_____
Username:_____
Password:_____
Hint:_____
Notes:
_____
_____
_____

Website:_____
Username:_____
Password:_____
Hint:_____
Notes:
_____
_____
_____

Website:_____
Username:_____
Password:_____
Hint:_____
Notes:
_____
_____
_____

Website:_____
Username:_____
Password:_____
Hint:_____
Notes:
_____
_____

Website:_____
Username:_____
Password:_____
Hint:_____
Notes:

_____
_____
_____

Website:_____
Username:_____
Password:_____
Hint:_____
Notes:

_____
_____
_____

Website:_____
Username:_____
Password:_____
Hint:_____
Notes:

_____
_____
_____

Website:_____
Username:_____
Password:_____
Hint:_____
Notes:

_____
_____
_____

Website:_____
Username:_____
Password:_____
Hint:_____
Notes:

_____
_____

Website:_____
Username:_____
Password:_____
Hint:_____
Notes:

_____
_____
_____

Website:_____
Username:_____
Password:_____
Hint:_____
Notes:

_____
_____
_____

Website:_____
Username:_____
Password:_____
Hint:_____
Notes:

_____
_____
_____

Website:_____
Username:_____
Password:_____
Hint:_____
Notes:

_____
_____
_____

Website:_____
Username:_____
Password:_____
Hint:_____
Notes:

_____
_____

Website:_____
Username:_____
Password:_____
Hint:_____
Notes:

_____
_____
_____

Website:_____
Username:_____
Password:_____
Hint:_____
Notes:

_____
_____
_____

Website:_____
Username:_____
Password:_____
Hint:_____
Notes:

_____
_____
_____

Website:_____
Username:_____
Password:_____
Hint:_____
Notes:

_____
_____
_____

Website:_____
Username:_____
Password:_____
Hint:_____
Notes:

_____
_____

Website:_____
Username:_____
Password:_____
Hint:_____
Notes:

_____
_____
_____

Website:_____
Username:_____
Password:_____
Hint:_____
Notes:

_____
_____
_____

Website:_____
Username:_____
Password:_____
Hint:_____
Notes:

_____
_____
_____

Website:_____
Username:_____
Password:_____
Hint:_____
Notes:

_____
_____
_____

Website:_____
Username:_____
Password:_____
Hint:_____
Notes:

_____
_____

Website:_____
Username:_____
Password:_____
Hint:_____
Notes:

_____
_____
_____

Website:_____
Username:_____
Password:_____
Hint:_____
Notes:

_____
_____
_____

Website:_____
Username:_____
Password:_____
Hint:_____
Notes:

_____
_____
_____

Website:_____
Username:_____
Password:_____
Hint:_____
Notes:

_____
_____
_____

Website:_____
Username:_____
Password:_____
Hint:_____
Notes:

_____
_____

Website:_____

Username:_____

Password:_____

Hint:_____

Notes:

_____

_____

_____

Website:_____

Username:_____

Password:_____

Hint:_____

Notes:

_____

_____

_____

Website:_____

Username:_____

Password:_____

Hint:_____

Notes:

_____

_____

_____

Website:_____

Username:_____

Password:_____

Hint:_____

Notes:

_____

_____

_____

Website:_____

Username:_____

Password:_____

Hint:_____

Notes:

_____

_____

Website:_____

Username:_____

Password:_____

Hint:_____

Notes:

_____

_____

_____

Website:_____

Username:_____

Password:_____

Hint:_____

Notes:

_____

_____

_____

Website:_____

Username:_____

Password:_____

Hint:_____

Notes:

_____

_____

_____

Website:_____

Username:_____

Password:_____

Hint:_____

Notes:

_____

_____

_____

Website:_____

Username:_____

Password:_____

Hint:_____

Notes:

_____

_____

Website:_____
Username:_____
Password:_____
Hint:_____
Notes:

_____
_____
_____

Website:_____
Username:_____
Password:_____
Hint:_____
Notes:

_____
_____
_____

Website:_____
Username:_____
Password:_____
Hint:_____
Notes:

_____
_____
_____

Website:_____
Username:_____
Password:_____
Hint:_____
Notes:

_____
_____
_____

Website:_____
Username:_____
Password:_____
Hint:_____
Notes:

_____
_____

Website:_____
Username:_____
Password:_____
Hint:_____
Notes:

_____
_____
_____

Website:_____
Username:_____
Password:_____
Hint:_____
Notes:

_____
_____
_____

Website:_____
Username:_____
Password:_____
Hint:_____
Notes:

_____
_____
_____

Website:_____
Username:_____
Password:_____
Hint:_____
Notes:

_____
_____
_____

Website:_____
Username:_____
Password:_____
Hint:_____
Notes:

_____
_____

Website:_____
Username:_____
Password:_____
Hint:_____
Notes:

_____
_____
_____

Website:_____
Username:_____
Password:_____
Hint:_____
Notes:

_____
_____
_____

Website:_____
Username:_____
Password:_____
Hint:_____
Notes:

_____
_____
_____

Website:_____
Username:_____
Password:_____
Hint:_____
Notes:

_____
_____
_____

Website:_____
Username:_____
Password:_____
Hint:_____
Notes:

_____
_____

Website:_____
Username:_____
Password:_____
Hint:_____
Notes:

_____
_____
_____

Website:_____
Username:_____
Password:_____
Hint:_____
Notes:

_____
_____
_____

Website:_____
Username:_____
Password:_____
Hint:_____
Notes:

_____
_____
_____

Website:_____
Username:_____
Password:_____
Hint:_____
Notes:

_____
_____
_____

Website:_____
Username:_____
Password:_____
Hint:_____
Notes:

_____
_____

Website:_____
Username:_____
Password:_____
Hint:_____
Notes:
_____
_____
_____

Website:_____
Username:_____
Password:_____
Hint:_____
Notes:
_____
_____
_____

Website:_____
Username:_____
Password:_____
Hint:_____
Notes:
_____
_____
_____

Website:_____
Username:_____
Password:_____
Hint:_____
Notes:
_____
_____
_____

Website:_____
Username:_____
Password:_____
Hint:_____
Notes:
_____
_____

Website:_____
Username:_____
Password:_____
Hint:_____
Notes:
_____
_____
_____

Website:_____
Username:_____
Password:_____
Hint:_____
Notes:
_____
_____
_____

Website:_____
Username:_____
Password:_____
Hint:_____
Notes:
_____
_____
_____

Website:_____
Username:_____
Password:_____
Hint:_____
Notes:
_____
_____
_____

Website:_____
Username:_____
Password:_____
Hint:_____
Notes:
_____
_____

Website:_____
Username:_____
Password:_____
Hint:_____
Notes:

_____
_____
_____

Website:_____
Username:_____
Password:_____
Hint:_____
Notes:

_____
_____
_____

Website:_____
Username:_____
Password:_____
Hint:_____
Notes:

_____
_____
_____

Website:_____
Username:_____
Password:_____
Hint:_____
Notes:

_____
_____
_____

Website:_____
Username:_____
Password:_____
Hint:_____
Notes:

_____
_____

Website:_____
Username:_____
Password:_____
Hint:_____
Notes:
_____
_____
_____

Website:_____
Username:_____
Password:_____
Hint:_____
Notes:
_____
_____
_____

Website:_____
Username:_____
Password:_____
Hint:_____
Notes:
_____
_____
_____

Website:_____
Username:_____
Password:_____
Hint:_____
Notes:
_____
_____
_____

Website:_____
Username:_____
Password:_____
Hint:_____
Notes:
_____
_____

Website:_____
Username:_____
Password:_____
Hint:_____
Notes:

_____
_____
_____

Website:_____
Username:_____
Password:_____
Hint:_____
Notes:

_____
_____
_____

Website:_____
Username:_____
Password:_____
Hint:_____
Notes:

_____
_____
_____

Website:_____
Username:_____
Password:_____
Hint:_____
Notes:

_____
_____
_____

Website:_____
Username:_____
Password:_____
Hint:_____
Notes:

_____
_____

Website:_____

Username:_____

Password:_____

Hint:_____

Notes:

_____

_____

_____

Website:_____

Username:_____

Password:_____

Hint:_____

Notes:

_____

_____

_____

Website:_____

Username:_____

Password:_____

Hint:_____

Notes:

_____

_____

_____

Website:_____

Username:_____

Password:_____

Hint:_____

Notes:

_____

_____

_____

Website:_____

Username:_____

Password:_____

Hint:_____

Notes:

_____

_____

Website:_____
Username:_____
Password:_____
Hint:_____
Notes:

_____
_____
_____

Website:_____
Username:_____
Password:_____
Hint:_____
Notes:

_____
_____
_____

Website:_____
Username:_____
Password:_____
Hint:_____
Notes:

_____
_____
_____

Website:_____
Username:_____
Password:_____
Hint:_____
Notes:

_____
_____
_____

Website:_____
Username:_____
Password:_____
Hint:_____
Notes:

_____
_____

Website:

Username:

Password:

Hint:

Notes:

Website:

Username:

Password:

Hint:

Notes:

Website:

Username:

Password:

Hint:

Notes:

Website:

Username:

Password:

Hint:

Notes:

Website:

Username:

Password:

Hint:

Notes:

Website:_____
Username:_____
Password:_____
Hint:_____
Notes:

_____
_____
_____

Website:_____
Username:_____
Password:_____
Hint:_____
Notes:

_____
_____
_____

Website:_____
Username:_____
Password:_____
Hint:_____
Notes:

_____
_____
_____

Website:_____
Username:_____
Password:_____
Hint:_____
Notes:

_____
_____
_____

Website:_____
Username:_____
Password:_____
Hint:_____
Notes:

_____
_____

Website:_____
Username:_____
Password:_____
Hint:_____
Notes:
_____
_____
_____

Website:_____
Username:_____
Password:_____
Hint:_____
Notes:
_____
_____
_____

Website:_____
Username:_____
Password:_____
Hint:_____
Notes:
_____
_____
_____

Website:_____
Username:_____
Password:_____
Hint:_____
Notes:
_____
_____
_____

Website:_____
Username:_____
Password:_____
Hint:_____
Notes:
_____
_____

Website:_____
Username:_____
Password:_____
Hint:_____
Notes:
_____
_____
_____

Website:_____
Username:_____
Password:_____
Hint:_____
Notes:
_____
_____
_____

Website:_____
Username:_____
Password:_____
Hint:_____
Notes:
_____
_____
_____

Website:_____
Username:_____
Password:_____
Hint:_____
Notes:
_____
_____
_____

Website:_____
Username:_____
Password:_____
Hint:_____
Notes:
_____
_____

Website:_____
Username:_____
Password:_____
Hint:_____
Notes:
_____
_____
_____

Website:_____
Username:_____
Password:_____
Hint:_____
Notes:
_____
_____
_____

Website:_____
Username:_____
Password:_____
Hint:_____
Notes:
_____
_____
_____

Website:_____
Username:_____
Password:_____
Hint:_____
Notes:
_____
_____
_____

Website:_____
Username:_____
Password:_____
Hint:_____
Notes:
_____
_____

Website:_____
Username:_____
Password:_____
Hint:_____
Notes:

_____
_____
_____

Website:_____
Username:_____
Password:_____
Hint:_____
Notes:

_____
_____
_____

Website:_____
Username:_____
Password:_____
Hint:_____
Notes:

_____
_____
_____

Website:_____
Username:_____
Password:_____
Hint:_____
Notes:

_____
_____
_____

Website:_____
Username:_____
Password:_____
Hint:_____
Notes:

_____
_____

Website:_____
Username:_____
Password:_____
Hint:_____
Notes:

_____
_____
_____

Website:_____
Username:_____
Password:_____
Hint:_____
Notes:

_____
_____
_____

Website:_____
Username:_____
Password:_____
Hint:_____
Notes:

_____
_____
_____

Website:_____
Username:_____
Password:_____
Hint:_____
Notes:

_____
_____
_____

Website:_____
Username:_____
Password:_____
Hint:_____
Notes:

_____
_____

Website:_____
Username:_____
Password:_____
Hint:_____
Notes:

_____
_____
_____

Website:_____
Username:_____
Password:_____
Hint:_____
Notes:

_____
_____
_____

Website:_____
Username:_____
Password:_____
Hint:_____
Notes:

_____
_____
_____

Website:_____
Username:_____
Password:_____
Hint:_____
Notes:

_____
_____
_____

Website:_____
Username:_____
Password:_____
Hint:_____
Notes:

_____
_____

Website:_____
Username:_____
Password:_____
Hint:_____
Notes:

_____
_____
_____

Website:_____
Username:_____
Password:_____
Hint:_____
Notes:

_____
_____
_____

Website:_____
Username:_____
Password:_____
Hint:_____
Notes:

_____
_____
_____

Website:_____
Username:_____
Password:_____
Hint:_____
Notes:

_____
_____
_____

Website:_____
Username:_____
Password:_____
Hint:_____
Notes:

_____
_____

Website:_____
Username:_____
Password:_____
Hint:_____
Notes:
_____
_____
_____

Website:_____
Username:_____
Password:_____
Hint:_____
Notes:
_____
_____
_____

Website:_____
Username:_____
Password:_____
Hint:_____
Notes:
_____
_____
_____

Website:_____
Username:_____
Password:_____
Hint:_____
Notes:
_____
_____
_____

Website:_____
Username:_____
Password:_____
Hint:_____
Notes:
_____
_____

Website:_____
Username:_____
Password:_____
Hint:_____
Notes:

_____
_____
_____

Website:_____
Username:_____
Password:_____
Hint:_____
Notes:

_____
_____
_____

Website:_____
Username:_____
Password:_____
Hint:_____
Notes:

_____
_____
_____

Website:_____
Username:_____
Password:_____
Hint:_____
Notes:

_____
_____
_____

Website:_____
Username:_____
Password:_____
Hint:_____
Notes:

_____
_____

Website:_____
Username:_____
Password:_____
Hint:_____
Notes:

_____
_____
_____

Website:_____
Username:_____
Password:_____
Hint:_____
Notes:

_____
_____
_____

Website:_____
Username:_____
Password:_____
Hint:_____
Notes:

_____
_____
_____

Website:_____
Username:_____
Password:_____
Hint:_____
Notes:

_____
_____
_____

Website:_____
Username:_____
Password:_____
Hint:_____
Notes:

_____
_____

Website:_____
Username:_____
Password:_____
Hint:_____
Notes:

_____
_____
_____

Website:_____
Username:_____
Password:_____
Hint:_____
Notes:

_____
_____
_____

Website:_____
Username:_____
Password:_____
Hint:_____
Notes:

_____
_____
_____

Website:_____
Username:_____
Password:_____
Hint:_____
Notes:

_____
_____
_____

Website:_____
Username:_____
Password:_____
Hint:_____
Notes:

_____
_____

Website:_____
Username:_____
Password:_____
Hint:_____
Notes:

_____
_____
_____

Website:_____
Username:_____
Password:_____
Hint:_____
Notes:

_____
_____
_____

Website:_____
Username:_____
Password:_____
Hint:_____
Notes:

_____
_____
_____

Website:_____
Username:_____
Password:_____
Hint:_____
Notes:

_____
_____
_____

Website:_____
Username:_____
Password:_____
Hint:_____
Notes:

_____
_____

Website:_____
Username:_____
Password:_____
Hint:_____
Notes:
_____
_____
_____

Website:_____
Username:_____
Password:_____
Hint:_____
Notes:
_____
_____
_____

Website:_____
Username:_____
Password:_____
Hint:_____
Notes:
_____
_____
_____

Website:_____
Username:_____
Password:_____
Hint:_____
Notes:
_____
_____
_____

Website:_____
Username:_____
Password:_____
Hint:_____
Notes:
_____
_____

Website:_____
Username:_____
Password:_____
Hint:_____
Notes:

_____
_____
_____

Website:_____
Username:_____
Password:_____
Hint:_____
Notes:

_____
_____
_____

Website:_____
Username:_____
Password:_____
Hint:_____
Notes:

_____
_____
_____

Website:_____
Username:_____
Password:_____
Hint:_____
Notes:

_____
_____
_____

Website:_____
Username:_____
Password:_____
Hint:_____
Notes:

_____
_____

Website:_____
Username:_____
Password:_____
Hint:_____
Notes:
_____
_____
_____

Website:_____
Username:_____
Password:_____
Hint:_____
Notes:
_____
_____
_____

Website:_____
Username:_____
Password:_____
Hint:_____
Notes:
_____
_____
_____

Website:_____
Username:_____
Password:_____
Hint:_____
Notes:
_____
_____
_____

Website:_____
Username:_____
Password:_____
Hint:_____
Notes:
_____
_____

Website:_____

Username:_____

Password:_____

Hint:_____

Notes:

_____

_____

_____

Website:_____

Username:_____

Password:_____

Hint:_____

Notes:

_____

_____

_____

Website:_____

Username:_____

Password:_____

Hint:_____

Notes:

_____

_____

_____

Website:_____

Username:_____

Password:_____

Hint:_____

Notes:

_____

_____

_____

Website:_____

Username:_____

Password:_____

Hint:_____

Notes:

_____

_____

Website:_____
Username:_____
Password:_____
Hint:_____
Notes:
_____
_____
_____

Website:_____
Username:_____
Password:_____
Hint:_____
Notes:
_____
_____
_____

Website:_____
Username:_____
Password:_____
Hint:_____
Notes:
_____
_____
_____

Website:_____
Username:_____
Password:_____
Hint:_____
Notes:
_____
_____
_____

Website:_____
Username:_____
Password:_____
Hint:_____
Notes:
_____
_____
_____

Website:_____
Username:_____
Password:_____
Hint:_____
Notes:
_____
_____
_____

Website:_____
Username:_____
Password:_____
Hint:_____
Notes:
_____
_____
_____

Website:_____
Username:_____
Password:_____
Hint:_____
Notes:
_____
_____
_____

Website:_____
Username:_____
Password:_____
Hint:_____
Notes:
_____
_____
_____

Website:_____
Username:_____
Password:_____
Hint:_____
Notes:
_____
_____

Website:_____
Username:_____
Password:_____
Hint:_____
Notes:

_____
_____
_____

Website:_____
Username:_____
Password:_____
Hint:_____
Notes:

_____
_____
_____

Website:_____
Username:_____
Password:_____
Hint:_____
Notes:

_____
_____
_____

Website:_____
Username:_____
Password:_____
Hint:_____
Notes:

_____
_____
_____

Website:_____
Username:_____
Password:_____
Hint:_____
Notes:

_____
_____
_____

Website:_____
Username:_____
Password:_____
Hint:_____
Notes:

_____
_____
_____

Website:_____
Username:_____
Password:_____
Hint:_____
Notes:

_____
_____
_____

Website:_____
Username:_____
Password:_____
Hint:_____
Notes:

_____
_____
_____

Website:_____
Username:_____
Password:_____
Hint:_____
Notes:

_____
_____
_____

Website:_____
Username:_____
Password:_____
Hint:_____
Notes:

_____
_____

Website:_____
Username:_____
Password:_____
Hint:_____
Notes:

_____
_____
_____

Website:_____
Username:_____
Password:_____
Hint:_____
Notes:

_____
_____
_____

Website:_____
Username:_____
Password:_____
Hint:_____
Notes:

_____
_____
_____

Website:_____
Username:_____
Password:_____
Hint:_____
Notes:

_____
_____
_____

Website:_____
Username:_____
Password:_____
Hint:_____
Notes:

_____
_____
_____

Website:_____
Username:_____
Password:_____
Hint:_____
Notes:
_____
_____
_____

Website:_____
Username:_____
Password:_____
Hint:_____
Notes:
_____
_____
_____

Website:_____
Username:_____
Password:_____
Hint:_____
Notes:
_____
_____
_____

Website:_____
Username:_____
Password:_____
Hint:_____
Notes:
_____
_____
_____

Website:_____
Username:_____
Password:_____
Hint:_____
Notes:
_____
_____

Website:_____

Username:_____

Password:_____

Hint:_____

Notes:

_____

_____

_____

Website:_____

Username:_____

Password:_____

Hint:_____

Notes:

_____

_____

_____

Website:_____

Username:_____

Password:_____

Hint:_____

Notes:

_____

_____

_____

Website:_____

Username:_____

Password:_____

Hint:_____

Notes:

_____

_____

_____

Website:_____

Username:_____

Password:_____

Hint:_____

Notes:

_____

_____

Website:_____
Username:_____
Password:_____
Hint:_____
Notes:

_____
_____
_____

Website:_____
Username:_____
Password:_____
Hint:_____
Notes:

_____
_____
_____

Website:_____
Username:_____
Password:_____
Hint:_____
Notes:

_____
_____
_____

Website:_____
Username:_____
Password:_____
Hint:_____
Notes:

_____
_____
_____

Website:_____
Username:_____
Password:_____
Hint:_____
Notes:

_____
_____

Website:_____
Username:_____
Password:_____
Hint:_____
Notes:
_____
_____
_____

Website:_____
Username:_____
Password:_____
Hint:_____
Notes:
_____
_____
_____

Website:_____
Username:_____
Password:_____
Hint:_____
Notes:
_____
_____
_____

Website:_____
Username:_____
Password:_____
Hint:_____
Notes:
_____
_____
_____

Website:_____
Username:_____
Password:_____
Hint:_____
Notes:
_____
_____

Website:_____

Username:_____

Password:_____

Hint:_____

Notes:

_____

_____

_____

Website:_____

Username:_____

Password:_____

Hint:_____

Notes:

_____

_____

_____

Website:_____

Username:_____

Password:_____

Hint:_____

Notes:

_____

_____

_____

Website:_____

Username:_____

Password:_____

Hint:_____

Notes:

_____

_____

_____

Website:_____

Username:_____

Password:_____

Hint:_____

Notes:

_____

_____

Website:_____
Username:_____
Password:_____
Hint:_____
Notes:

_____
_____
_____

Website:_____
Username:_____
Password:_____
Hint:_____
Notes:

_____
_____
_____

Website:_____
Username:_____
Password:_____
Hint:_____
Notes:

_____
_____
_____

Website:_____
Username:_____
Password:_____
Hint:_____
Notes:

_____
_____
_____

Website:_____
Username:_____
Password:_____
Hint:_____
Notes:

_____
_____
_____

Website:_____
Username:_____
Password:_____
Hint:_____
Notes:

_____
_____
_____

Website:_____
Username:_____
Password:_____
Hint:_____
Notes:

_____
_____
_____

Website:_____
Username:_____
Password:_____
Hint:_____
Notes:

_____
_____
_____

Website:_____
Username:_____
Password:_____
Hint:_____
Notes:

_____
_____
_____

Website:_____
Username:_____
Password:_____
Hint:_____
Notes:

_____
_____

Website:_____
Username:_____
Password:_____
Hint:_____
Notes:
_____
_____
_____

Website:_____
Username:_____
Password:_____
Hint:_____
Notes:
_____
_____
_____

Website:_____
Username:_____
Password:_____
Hint:_____
Notes:
_____
_____
_____

Website:_____
Username:_____
Password:_____
Hint:_____
Notes:
_____
_____
_____

Website:_____
Username:_____
Password:_____
Hint:_____
Notes:
_____
_____
_____

Website:_____
Username:_____
Password:_____
Hint:_____
Notes:

_____
_____
_____

Website:_____
Username:_____
Password:_____
Hint:_____
Notes:

_____
_____
_____

Website:_____
Username:_____
Password:_____
Hint:_____
Notes:

_____
_____
_____

Website:_____
Username:_____
Password:_____
Hint:_____
Notes:

_____
_____
_____

Website:_____
Username:_____
Password:_____
Hint:_____
Notes:

_____
_____

Website:_____
Username:_____
Password:_____
Hint:_____
Notes:

_____
_____
_____

Website:_____
Username:_____
Password:_____
Hint:_____
Notes:

_____
_____
_____

Website:_____
Username:_____
Password:_____
Hint:_____
Notes:

_____
_____
_____

Website:_____
Username:_____
Password:_____
Hint:_____
Notes:

_____
_____
_____

Website:_____
Username:_____
Password:_____
Hint:_____
Notes:

_____
_____

Website:_____
Username:_____
Password:_____
Hint:_____
Notes:
_____
_____
_____

Website:_____
Username:_____
Password:_____
Hint:_____
Notes:
_____
_____
_____

Website:_____
Username:_____
Password:_____
Hint:_____
Notes:
_____
_____
_____

Website:_____
Username:_____
Password:_____
Hint:_____
Notes:
_____
_____
_____

Website:_____
Username:_____
Password:_____
Hint:_____
Notes:
_____
_____

Website:_____
Username:_____
Password:_____
Hint:_____
Notes:

_____
_____
_____

Website:_____
Username:_____
Password:_____
Hint:_____
Notes:

_____
_____
_____

Website:_____
Username:_____
Password:_____
Hint:_____
Notes:

_____
_____
_____

Website:_____
Username:_____
Password:_____
Hint:_____
Notes:

_____
_____
_____

Website:_____
Username:_____
Password:_____
Hint:_____
Notes:

_____
_____

Website:_____
Username:_____
Password:_____
Hint:_____
Notes:
_____
_____
_____

Website:_____
Username:_____
Password:_____
Hint:_____
Notes:
_____
_____
_____

Website:_____
Username:_____
Password:_____
Hint:_____
Notes:
_____
_____
_____

Website:_____
Username:_____
Password:_____
Hint:_____
Notes:
_____
_____
_____

Website:_____
Username:_____
Password:_____
Hint:_____
Notes:
_____
_____

Website:_____
Username:_____
Password:_____
Hint:_____
Notes:

_____
_____
_____

Website:_____
Username:_____
Password:_____
Hint:_____
Notes:

_____
_____
_____

Website:_____
Username:_____
Password:_____
Hint:_____
Notes:

_____
_____
_____

Website:_____
Username:_____
Password:_____
Hint:_____
Notes:

_____
_____
_____

Website:_____
Username:_____
Password:_____
Hint:_____
Notes:

_____
_____

Website:_____
Username:_____
Password:_____
Hint:_____
Notes:

_____
_____
_____

Website:_____
Username:_____
Password:_____
Hint:_____
Notes:

_____
_____
_____

Website:_____
Username:_____
Password:_____
Hint:_____
Notes:

_____
_____
_____

Website:_____
Username:_____
Password:_____
Hint:_____
Notes:

_____
_____
_____

Website:_____
Username:_____
Password:_____
Hint:_____
Notes:

_____
_____

Website:_____

Username:_____

Password:_____

Hint:_____

Notes:

_____

_____

_____

Website:_____

Username:_____

Password:_____

Hint:_____

Notes:

_____

_____

_____

Website:_____

Username:_____

Password:_____

Hint:_____

Notes:

_____

_____

_____

Website:_____

Username:_____

Password:_____

Hint:_____

Notes:

_____

_____

_____

Website:_____

Username:_____

Password:_____

Hint:_____

Notes:

_____

_____

Website: _____
Username: _____
Password: _____
Hint: _____
Notes:
_____
_____
_____

Website: _____
Username: _____
Password: _____
Hint: _____
Notes:
_____
_____
_____

Website: _____
Username: _____
Password: _____
Hint: _____
Notes:
_____
_____
_____

Website: _____
Username: _____
Password: _____
Hint: _____
Notes:
_____
_____
_____

Website: _____
Username: _____
Password: _____
Hint: _____
Notes:
_____
_____

Website:_____
Username:_____
Password:_____
Hint:_____
Notes:

_____
_____
_____

Website:_____
Username:_____
Password:_____
Hint:_____
Notes:

_____
_____
_____

Website:_____
Username:_____
Password:_____
Hint:_____
Notes:

_____
_____
_____

Website:_____
Username:_____
Password:_____
Hint:_____
Notes:

_____
_____
_____

Website:_____
Username:_____
Password:_____
Hint:_____
Notes:

_____
_____
_____

Website:_____
Username:_____
Password:_____
Hint:_____
Notes:

_____
_____
_____

Website:_____
Username:_____
Password:_____
Hint:_____
Notes:

_____
_____
_____

Website:_____
Username:_____
Password:_____
Hint:_____
Notes:

_____
_____
_____

Website:_____
Username:_____
Password:_____
Hint:_____
Notes:

_____
_____
_____

Website:_____
Username:_____
Password:_____
Hint:_____
Notes:

_____
_____

Website:_____
Username:_____
Password:_____
Hint:_____
Notes:

_____
_____
_____

Website:_____
Username:_____
Password:_____
Hint:_____
Notes:

_____
_____
_____

Website:_____
Username:_____
Password:_____
Hint:_____
Notes:

_____
_____
_____

Website:_____
Username:_____
Password:_____
Hint:_____
Notes:

_____
_____
_____

Website:_____
Username:_____
Password:_____
Hint:_____
Notes:

_____
_____

Website:_____
Username:_____
Password:_____
Hint:_____
Notes:
_____
_____
_____

Website:_____
Username:_____
Password:_____
Hint:_____
Notes:
_____
_____
_____

Website:_____
Username:_____
Password:_____
Hint:_____
Notes:
_____
_____
_____

Website:_____
Username:_____
Password:_____
Hint:_____
Notes:
_____
_____
_____

Website:_____
Username:_____
Password:_____
Hint:_____
Notes:
_____
_____

Website:_____
Username:_____
Password:_____
Hint:_____
Notes:

_____
_____
_____

Website:_____
Username:_____
Password:_____
Hint:_____
Notes:

_____
_____
_____

Website:_____
Username:_____
Password:_____
Hint:_____
Notes:

_____
_____
_____

Website:_____
Username:_____
Password:_____
Hint:_____
Notes:

_____
_____
_____

Website:_____
Username:_____
Password:_____
Hint:_____
Notes:

_____
_____

Website:_____
Username:_____
Password:_____
Hint:_____
Notes:

_____
_____
_____

Website:_____
Username:_____
Password:_____
Hint:_____
Notes:

_____
_____
_____

Website:_____
Username:_____
Password:_____
Hint:_____
Notes:

_____
_____
_____

Website:_____
Username:_____
Password:_____
Hint:_____
Notes:

_____
_____
_____

Website:_____
Username:_____
Password:_____
Hint:_____
Notes:

_____
_____

Website:_____
Username:_____
Password:_____
Hint:_____
Notes:

_____
_____
_____

Website:_____
Username:_____
Password:_____
Hint:_____
Notes:

_____
_____
_____

Website:_____
Username:_____
Password:_____
Hint:_____
Notes:

_____
_____
_____

Website:_____
Username:_____
Password:_____
Hint:_____
Notes:

_____
_____
_____

Website:_____
Username:_____
Password:_____
Hint:_____
Notes:

_____
_____

Website:_____
Username:_____
Password:_____
Hint:_____
Notes:

_____
_____
_____

Website:_____
Username:_____
Password:_____
Hint:_____
Notes:

_____
_____
_____

Website:_____
Username:_____
Password:_____
Hint:_____
Notes:

_____
_____
_____

Website:_____
Username:_____
Password:_____
Hint:_____
Notes:

_____
_____
_____

Website:_____
Username:_____
Password:_____
Hint:_____
Notes:

_____
_____

Website:_____

Username:_____

Password:_____

Hint:_____

Notes:

_____

_____

_____

Website:_____

Username:_____

Password:_____

Hint:_____

Notes:

_____

_____

_____

Website:_____

Username:_____

Password:_____

Hint:_____

Notes:

_____

_____

_____

Website:_____

Username:_____

Password:_____

Hint:_____

Notes:

_____

_____

_____

Website:_____

Username:_____

Password:_____

Hint:_____

Notes:

_____

_____

_____

Website:_____
Username:_____
Password:_____
Hint:_____
Notes:

_____
_____
_____

Website:_____
Username:_____
Password:_____
Hint:_____
Notes:

_____
_____
_____

Website:_____
Username:_____
Password:_____
Hint:_____
Notes:

_____
_____
_____

Website:_____
Username:_____
Password:_____
Hint:_____
Notes:

_____
_____
_____

Website:_____
Username:_____
Password:_____
Hint:_____
Notes:

_____
_____

Website:_____
Username:_____
Password:_____
Hint:_____
Notes:

_____
_____
_____

Website:_____
Username:_____
Password:_____
Hint:_____
Notes:

_____
_____
_____

Website:_____
Username:_____
Password:_____
Hint:_____
Notes:

_____
_____
_____

Website:_____
Username:_____
Password:_____
Hint:_____
Notes:

_____
_____
_____

Website:_____
Username:_____
Password:_____
Hint:_____
Notes:

_____
_____

Website:_____

Username:_____

Password:_____

Hint:_____

Notes:

_____

_____

_____

Website:_____

Username:_____

Password:_____

Hint:_____

Notes:

_____

_____

_____

Website:_____

Username:_____

Password:_____

Hint:_____

Notes:

_____

_____

_____

Website:_____

Username:_____

Password:_____

Hint:_____

Notes:

_____

_____

_____

Website:_____

Username:_____

Password:_____

Hint:_____

Notes:

_____

_____

Website:_____
Username:_____
Password:_____
Hint:_____
Notes:

_____
_____
_____

Website:_____
Username:_____
Password:_____
Hint:_____
Notes:

_____
_____
_____

Website:_____
Username:_____
Password:_____
Hint:_____
Notes:

_____
_____
_____

Website:_____
Username:_____
Password:_____
Hint:_____
Notes:

_____
_____
_____

Website:_____
Username:_____
Password:_____
Hint:_____
Notes:

_____
_____

Website:_____
Username:_____
Password:_____
Hint:_____
Notes:

_____
_____
_____

Website:_____
Username:_____
Password:_____
Hint:_____
Notes:

_____
_____
_____

Website:_____
Username:_____
Password:_____
Hint:_____
Notes:

_____
_____
_____

Website:_____
Username:_____
Password:_____
Hint:_____
Notes:

_____
_____
_____

Website:_____
Username:_____
Password:_____
Hint:_____
Notes:

_____
_____

Website:_____
Username:_____
Password:_____
Hint:_____
Notes:

_____
_____
_____

Website:_____
Username:_____
Password:_____
Hint:_____
Notes:

_____
_____
_____

Website:_____
Username:_____
Password:_____
Hint:_____
Notes:

_____
_____
_____

Website:_____
Username:_____
Password:_____
Hint:_____
Notes:

_____
_____
_____

Website:_____
Username:_____
Password:_____
Hint:_____
Notes:

_____
_____
_____

Website:_____
Username:_____
Password:_____
Hint:_____
Notes:
_____
_____
_____

Website:_____
Username:_____
Password:_____
Hint:_____
Notes:
_____
_____
_____

Website:_____
Username:_____
Password:_____
Hint:_____
Notes:
_____
_____
_____

Website:_____
Username:_____
Password:_____
Hint:_____
Notes:
_____
_____
_____

Website:_____
Username:_____
Password:_____
Hint:_____
Notes:
_____
_____

Website:_____
Username:_____
Password:_____
Hint:_____
Notes:
_____
_____
_____

Website:_____
Username:_____
Password:_____
Hint:_____
Notes:
_____
_____
_____

Website:_____
Username:_____
Password:_____
Hint:_____
Notes:
_____
_____
_____

Website:_____
Username:_____
Password:_____
Hint:_____
Notes:
_____
_____
_____

Website:_____
Username:_____
Password:_____
Hint:_____
Notes:
_____
_____

Website:_____

Username:_____

Password:_____

Hint:_____

Notes:

_____

_____

_____

Website:_____

Username:_____

Password:_____

Hint:_____

Notes:

_____

_____

_____

Website:_____

Username:_____

Password:_____

Hint:_____

Notes:

_____

_____

_____

Website:_____

Username:_____

Password:_____

Hint:_____

Notes:

_____

_____

_____

Website:_____

Username:_____

Password:_____

Hint:_____

Notes:

_____

_____

Website:_____
Username:_____
Password:_____
Hint:_____
Notes:
_____
_____
_____

Website:_____
Username:_____
Password:_____
Hint:_____
Notes:
_____
_____
_____

Website:_____
Username:_____
Password:_____
Hint:_____
Notes:
_____
_____
_____

Website:_____
Username:_____
Password:_____
Hint:_____
Notes:
_____
_____
_____

Website:_____
Username:_____
Password:_____
Hint:_____
Notes:
_____
_____

Website:_____
Username:_____
Password:_____
Hint:_____
Notes:

_____
_____
_____

Website:_____
Username:_____
Password:_____
Hint:_____
Notes:

_____
_____
_____

Website:_____
Username:_____
Password:_____
Hint:_____
Notes:

_____
_____
_____

Website:_____
Username:_____
Password:_____
Hint:_____
Notes:

_____
_____
_____

Website:_____
Username:_____
Password:_____
Hint:_____
Notes:

_____
_____

Website:_____
Username:_____
Password:_____
Hint:_____
Notes:

_____
_____
_____

Website:_____
Username:_____
Password:_____
Hint:_____
Notes:

_____
_____
_____

Website:_____
Username:_____
Password:_____
Hint:_____
Notes:

_____
_____
_____

Website:_____
Username:_____
Password:_____
Hint:_____
Notes:

_____
_____
_____

Website:_____
Username:_____
Password:_____
Hint:_____
Notes:

_____
_____

Website:_____
Username:_____
Password:_____
Hint:_____
Notes:

_____
_____
_____

Website:_____
Username:_____
Password:_____
Hint:_____
Notes:

_____
_____
_____

Website:_____
Username:_____
Password:_____
Hint:_____
Notes:

_____
_____
_____

Website:_____
Username:_____
Password:_____
Hint:_____
Notes:

_____
_____
_____

Website:_____
Username:_____
Password:_____
Hint:_____
Notes:

_____
_____

Website:_____

Username:_____

Password:_____

Hint:_____

Notes:

_____

_____

_____

Website:_____

Username:_____

Password:_____

Hint:_____

Notes:

_____

_____

_____

Website:_____

Username:_____

Password:_____

Hint:_____

Notes:

_____

_____

_____

Website:_____

Username:_____

Password:_____

Hint:_____

Notes:

_____

_____

_____

Website:_____

Username:_____

Password:_____

Hint:_____

Notes:

_____

_____

Website:_____
Username:_____
Password:_____
Hint:_____
Notes:

_____
_____
_____

Website:_____
Username:_____
Password:_____
Hint:_____
Notes:

_____
_____
_____

Website:_____
Username:_____
Password:_____
Hint:_____
Notes:

_____
_____
_____

Website:_____
Username:_____
Password:_____
Hint:_____
Notes:

_____
_____
_____

Website:_____
Username:_____
Password:_____
Hint:_____
Notes:

_____
_____

Website:_____
Username:_____
Password:_____
Hint:_____
Notes:

_____
_____
_____

Website:_____
Username:_____
Password:_____
Hint:_____
Notes:

_____
_____
_____

Website:_____
Username:_____
Password:_____
Hint:_____
Notes:

_____
_____
_____

Website:_____
Username:_____
Password:_____
Hint:_____
Notes:

_____
_____
_____

Website:_____
Username:_____
Password:_____
Hint:_____
Notes:

_____
_____

Website:_____
Username:_____
Password:_____
Hint:_____
Notes:

_____
_____
_____

Website:_____
Username:_____
Password:_____
Hint:_____
Notes:

_____
_____
_____

Website:_____
Username:_____
Password:_____
Hint:_____
Notes:

_____
_____
_____

Website:_____
Username:_____
Password:_____
Hint:_____
Notes:

_____
_____
_____

Website:_____
Username:_____
Password:_____
Hint:_____
Notes:

_____
_____

Website:_____
Username:_____
Password:_____
Hint:_____
Notes:

_____
_____
_____

Website:_____
Username:_____
Password:_____
Hint:_____
Notes:

_____
_____
_____

Website:_____
Username:_____
Password:_____
Hint:_____
Notes:

_____
_____
_____

Website:_____
Username:_____
Password:_____
Hint:_____
Notes:

_____
_____
_____

Website:_____
Username:_____
Password:_____
Hint:_____
Notes:

_____
_____

Website:_____

Username:_____

Password:_____

Hint:_____

Notes:

_____

_____

_____

Website:_____

Username:_____

Password:_____

Hint:_____

Notes:

_____

_____

_____

Website:_____

Username:_____

Password:_____

Hint:_____

Notes:

_____

_____

_____

Website:_____

Username:_____

Password:_____

Hint:_____

Notes:

_____

_____

_____

Website:_____

Username:_____

Password:_____

Hint:_____

Notes:

_____

_____

Website:_____
Username:_____
Password:_____
Hint:_____
Notes:
_____
_____
_____

Website:_____
Username:_____
Password:_____
Hint:_____
Notes:
_____
_____
_____

Website:_____
Username:_____
Password:_____
Hint:_____
Notes:
_____
_____
_____

Website:_____
Username:_____
Password:_____
Hint:_____
Notes:
_____
_____
_____

Website:_____
Username:_____
Password:_____
Hint:_____
Notes:
_____
_____

Website:_____
Username:_____
Password:_____
Hint:_____
Notes:

_____
_____
_____

Website:_____
Username:_____
Password:_____
Hint:_____
Notes:

_____
_____
_____

Website:_____
Username:_____
Password:_____
Hint:_____
Notes:

_____
_____
_____

Website:_____
Username:_____
Password:_____
Hint:_____
Notes:

_____
_____
_____

Website:_____
Username:_____
Password:_____
Hint:_____
Notes:

_____
_____

Website:_____
Username:_____
Password:_____
Hint:_____
Notes:

_____
_____
_____

Website:_____
Username:_____
Password:_____
Hint:_____
Notes:

_____
_____
_____

Website:_____
Username:_____
Password:_____
Hint:_____
Notes:

_____
_____
_____

Website:_____
Username:_____
Password:_____
Hint:_____
Notes:

_____
_____
_____

Website:_____
Username:_____
Password:_____
Hint:_____
Notes:

_____
_____

Website:_____
Username:_____
Password:_____
Hint:_____
Notes:

_____
_____
_____

Website:_____
Username:_____
Password:_____
Hint:_____
Notes:

_____
_____
_____

Website:_____
Username:_____
Password:_____
Hint:_____
Notes:

_____
_____
_____

Website:_____
Username:_____
Password:_____
Hint:_____
Notes:

_____
_____
_____

Website:_____
Username:_____
Password:_____
Hint:_____
Notes:

_____
_____

Website:_____
Username:_____
Password:_____
Hint:_____
Notes:
_____
_____
_____

Website:_____
Username:_____
Password:_____
Hint:_____
Notes:
_____
_____
_____

Website:_____
Username:_____
Password:_____
Hint:_____
Notes:
_____
_____
_____

Website:_____
Username:_____
Password:_____
Hint:_____
Notes:
_____
_____
_____

Website:_____
Username:_____
Password:_____
Hint:_____
Notes:
_____
_____

Website:_____
Username:_____
Password:_____
Hint:_____
Notes:

_____
_____
_____

Website:_____
Username:_____
Password:_____
Hint:_____
Notes:

_____
_____
_____

Website:_____
Username:_____
Password:_____
Hint:_____
Notes:

_____
_____
_____

Website:_____
Username:_____
Password:_____
Hint:_____
Notes:

_____
_____
_____

Website:_____
Username:_____
Password:_____
Hint:_____
Notes:

_____
_____

Website:_____
Username:_____
Password:_____
Hint:_____
Notes:
_____
_____
_____

Website:_____
Username:_____
Password:_____
Hint:_____
Notes:
_____
_____
_____

Website:_____
Username:_____
Password:_____
Hint:_____
Notes:
_____
_____
_____

Website:_____
Username:_____
Password:_____
Hint:_____
Notes:
_____
_____
_____

Website:_____
Username:_____
Password:_____
Hint:_____
Notes:
_____
_____

Website:_____
Username:_____
Password:_____
Hint:_____
Notes:

_____
_____
_____

Website:_____
Username:_____
Password:_____
Hint:_____
Notes:

_____
_____
_____

Website:_____
Username:_____
Password:_____
Hint:_____
Notes:

_____
_____
_____

Website:_____
Username:_____
Password:_____
Hint:_____
Notes:

_____
_____
_____

Website:_____
Username:_____
Password:_____
Hint:_____
Notes:

_____
_____

www.ingramcontent.com/pod-product-compliance
Lightning Source LLC
Chambersburg PA
CBHW080738250626
47170CB00010B/2879